TROLL

THE ORIGINAL BOOK OF NORWEGIAN TROLLS

Illustrations: Rolf Lidberg • Text: Jan Lööf
Translated by: Pat Shaw

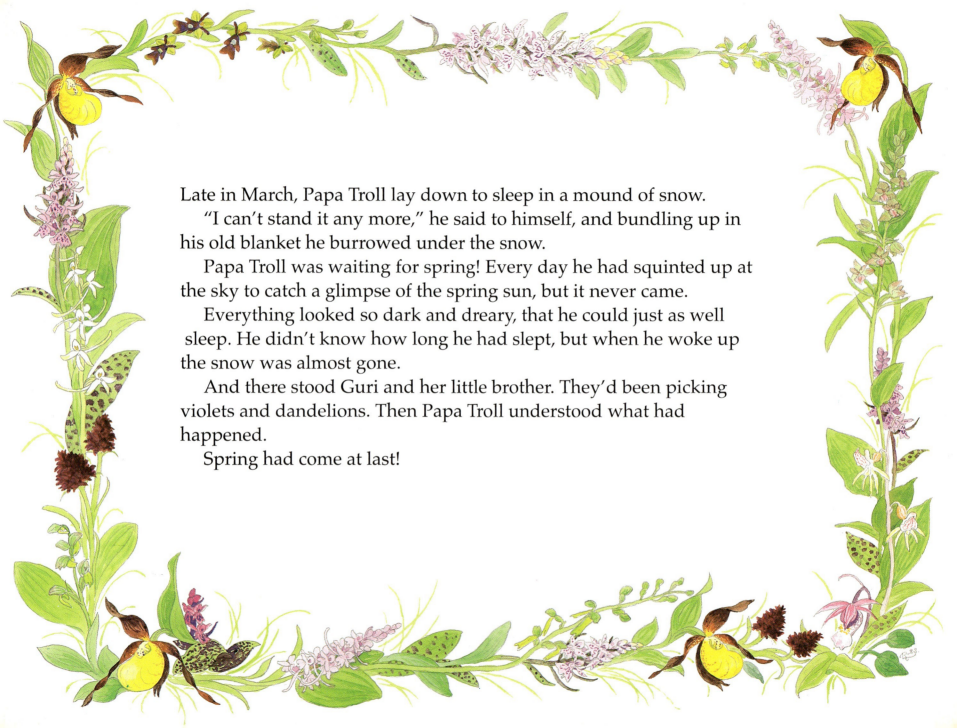

Late in March, Papa Troll lay down to sleep in a mound of snow.

"I can't stand it any more," he said to himself, and bundling up in his old blanket he burrowed under the snow.

Papa Troll was waiting for spring! Every day he had squinted up at the sky to catch a glimpse of the spring sun, but it never came.

Everything looked so dark and dreary, that he could just as well sleep. He didn't know how long he had slept, but when he woke up the snow was almost gone.

And there stood Guri and her little brother. They'd been picking violets and dandelions. Then Papa Troll understood what had happened.

Spring had come at last!

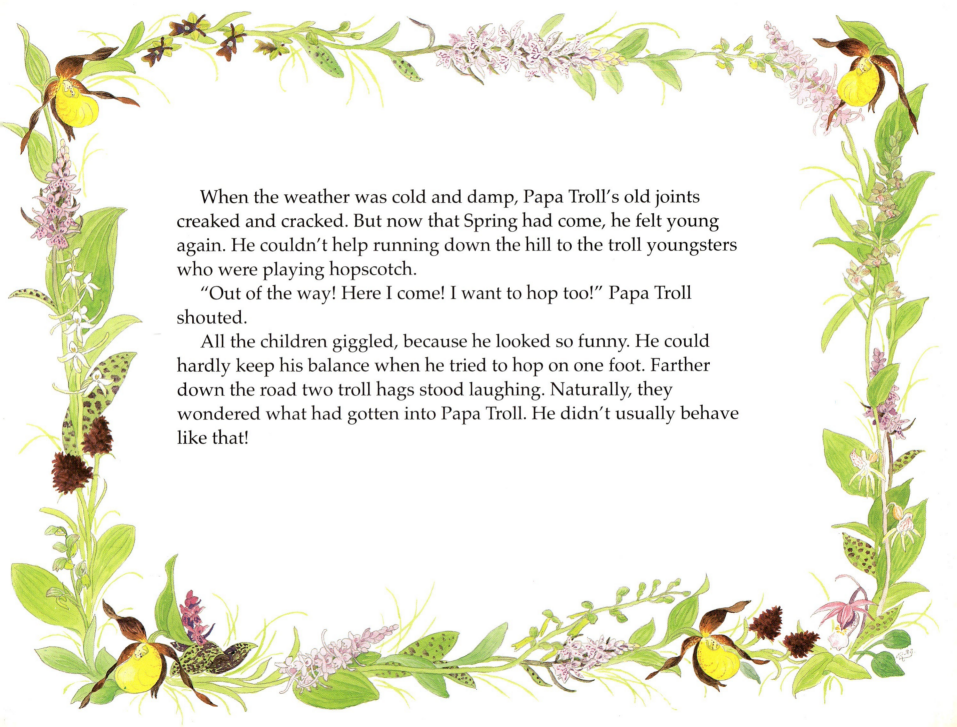

When the weather was cold and damp, Papa Troll's old joints creaked and cracked. But now that Spring had come, he felt young again. He couldn't help running down the hill to the troll youngsters who were playing hopscotch.

"Out of the way! Here I come! I want to hop too!" Papa Troll shouted.

All the children giggled, because he looked so funny. He could hardly keep his balance when he tried to hop on one foot. Farther down the road two troll hags stood laughing. Naturally, they wondered what had gotten into Papa Troll. He didn't usually behave like that!

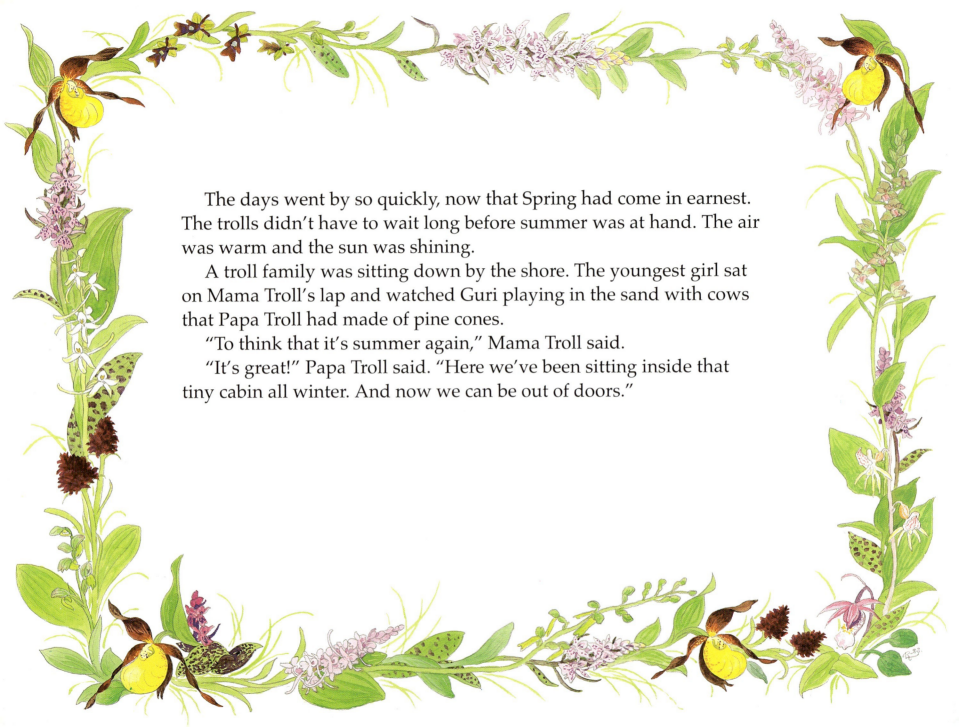

The days went by so quickly, now that Spring had come in earnest. The trolls didn't have to wait long before summer was at hand. The air was warm and the sun was shining.

A troll family was sitting down by the shore. The youngest girl sat on Mama Troll's lap and watched Guri playing in the sand with cows that Papa Troll had made of pine cones.

"To think that it's summer again," Mama Troll said.

"It's great!" Papa Troll said. "Here we've been sitting inside that tiny cabin all winter. And now we can be out of doors."

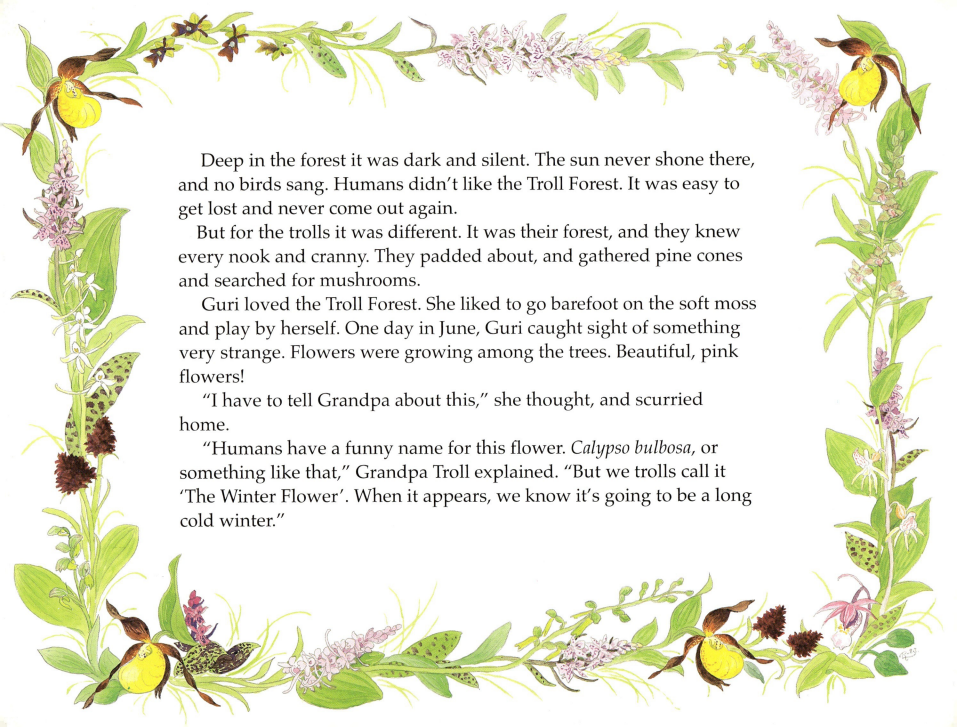

Deep in the forest it was dark and silent. The sun never shone there, and no birds sang. Humans didn't like the Troll Forest. It was easy to get lost and never come out again.

But for the trolls it was different. It was their forest, and they knew every nook and cranny. They padded about, and gathered pine cones and searched for mushrooms.

Guri loved the Troll Forest. She liked to go barefoot on the soft moss and play by herself. One day in June, Guri caught sight of something very strange. Flowers were growing among the trees. Beautiful, pink flowers!

"I have to tell Grandpa about this," she thought, and scurried home.

"Humans have a funny name for this flower. *Calypso bulbosa*, or something like that," Grandpa Troll explained. "But we trolls call it 'The Winter Flower'. When it appears, we know it's going to be a long cold winter."

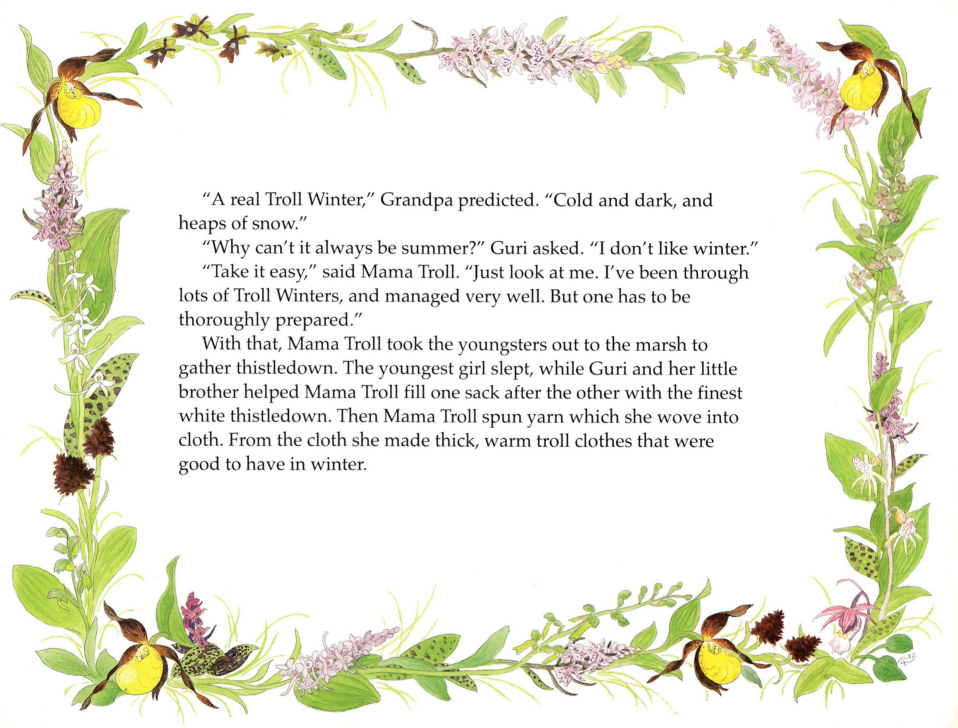

"A real Troll Winter," Grandpa predicted. "Cold and dark, and heaps of snow."

"Why can't it always be summer?" Guri asked. "I don't like winter."

"Take it easy," said Mama Troll. "Just look at me. I've been through lots of Troll Winters, and managed very well. But one has to be thoroughly prepared."

With that, Mama Troll took the youngsters out to the marsh to gather thistledown. The youngest girl slept, while Guri and her little brother helped Mama Troll fill one sack after the other with the finest white thistledown. Then Mama Troll spun yarn which she wove into cloth. From the cloth she made thick, warm troll clothes that were good to have in winter.

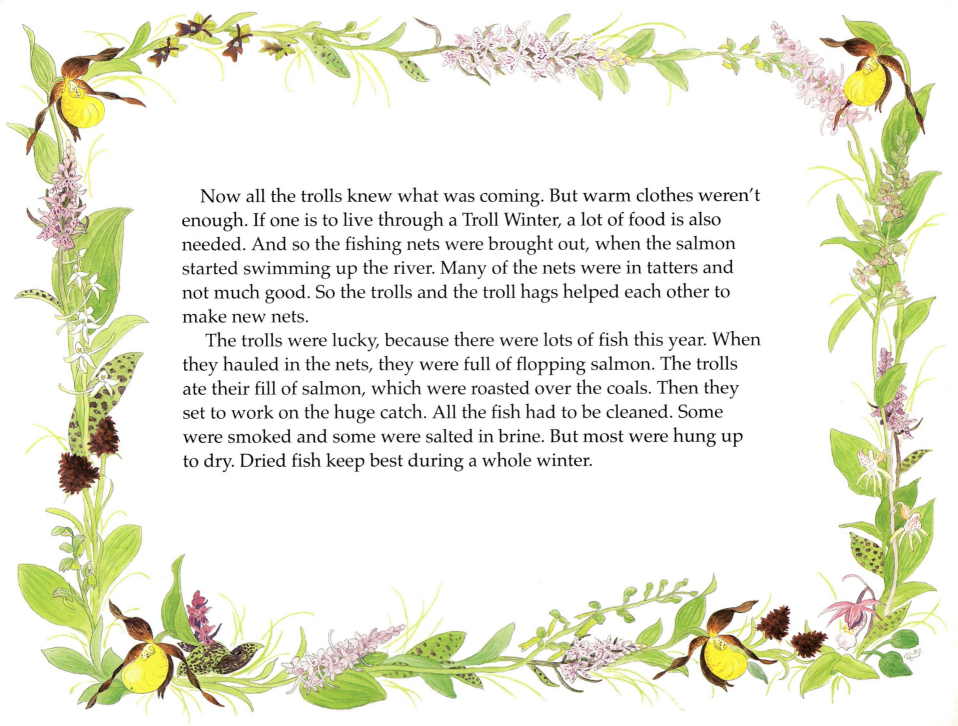

Now all the trolls knew what was coming. But warm clothes weren't enough. If one is to live through a Troll Winter, a lot of food is also needed. And so the fishing nets were brought out, when the salmon started swimming up the river. Many of the nets were in tatters and not much good. So the trolls and the troll hags helped each other to make new nets.

The trolls were lucky, because there were lots of fish this year. When they hauled in the nets, they were full of flopping salmon. The trolls ate their fill of salmon, which were roasted over the coals. Then they set to work on the huge catch. All the fish had to be cleaned. Some were smoked and some were salted in brine. But most were hung up to dry. Dried fish keep best during a whole winter.

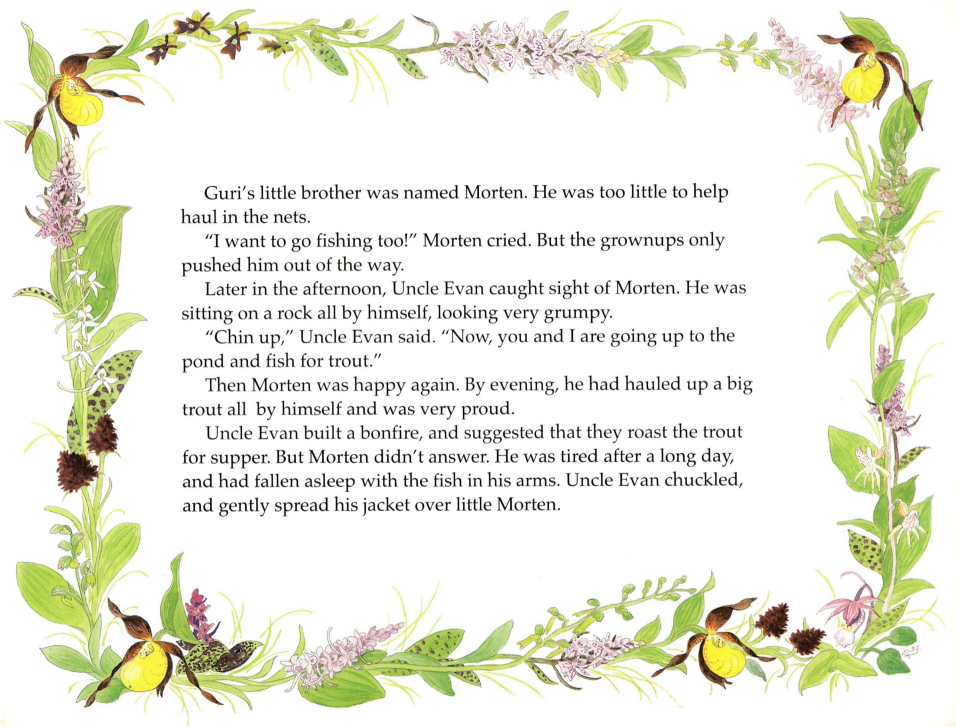

Guri's little brother was named Morten. He was too little to help haul in the nets.

"I want to go fishing too!" Morten cried. But the grownups only pushed him out of the way.

Later in the afternoon, Uncle Evan caught sight of Morten. He was sitting on a rock all by himself, looking very grumpy.

"Chin up," Uncle Evan said. "Now, you and I are going up to the pond and fish for trout."

Then Morten was happy again. By evening, he had hauled up a big trout all by himself and was very proud.

Uncle Evan built a bonfire, and suggested that they roast the trout for supper. But Morten didn't answer. He was tired after a long day, and had fallen asleep with the fish in his arms. Uncle Evan chuckled, and gently spread his jacket over little Morten.

Summer passed quickly. The days grew shorter and shorter, and autumn was drawing nigh. The forest was full of berries and mushrooms. And the trolls picked and gathered everything that could be eaten.

Morten was good at picking berries. So he thought. And so he was. At any rate, compared with Sara, his little sister. Because she ate all the berries she picked. In addition, she knocked over one of Grandma's baskets.

But it didn't matter, because all the trolls picked so many berries that the troll hags were busy making juice and jam for a whole week. The cellars were full of juice and jam. Here too, the trolls had potatoes and rutabagas. And in the woodsheds there were piles of dried fish. Now they had plenty.

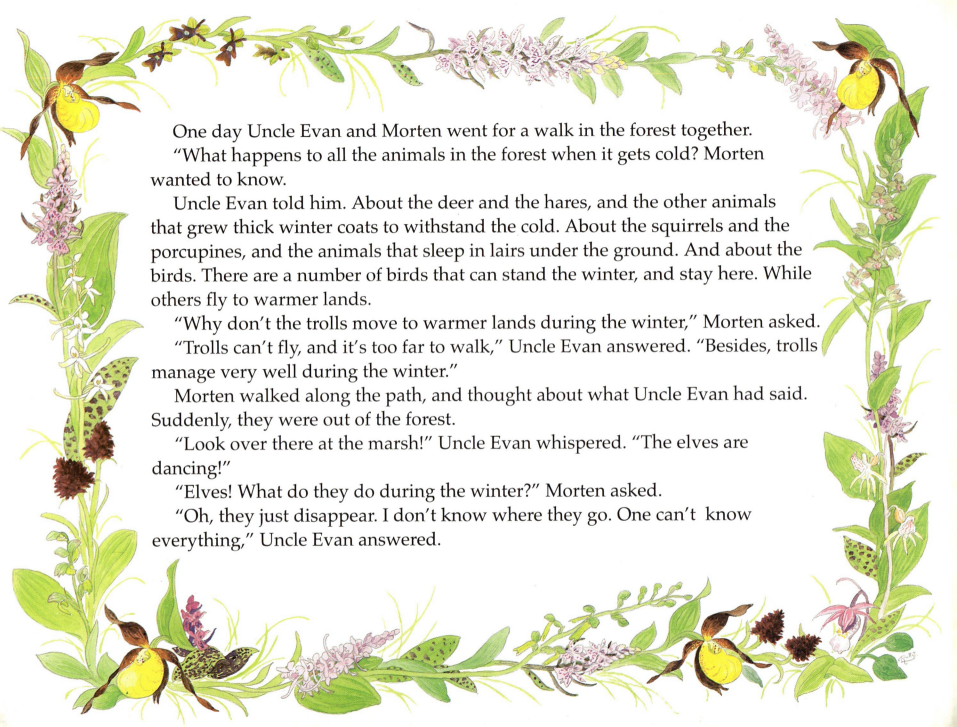

One day Uncle Evan and Morten went for a walk in the forest together.

"What happens to all the animals in the forest when it gets cold? Morten wanted to know.

Uncle Evan told him. About the deer and the hares, and the other animals that grew thick winter coats to withstand the cold. About the squirrels and the porcupines, and the animals that sleep in lairs under the ground. And about the birds. There are a number of birds that can stand the winter, and stay here. While others fly to warmer lands.

"Why don't the trolls move to warmer lands during the winter," Morten asked.

"Trolls can't fly, and it's too far to walk," Uncle Evan answered. "Besides, trolls manage very well during the winter."

Morten walked along the path, and thought about what Uncle Evan had said. Suddenly, they were out of the forest.

"Look over there at the marsh!" Uncle Evan whispered. "The elves are dancing!"

"Elves! What do they do during the winter?" Morten asked.

"Oh, they just disappear. I don't know where they go. One can't know everything," Uncle Evan answered.

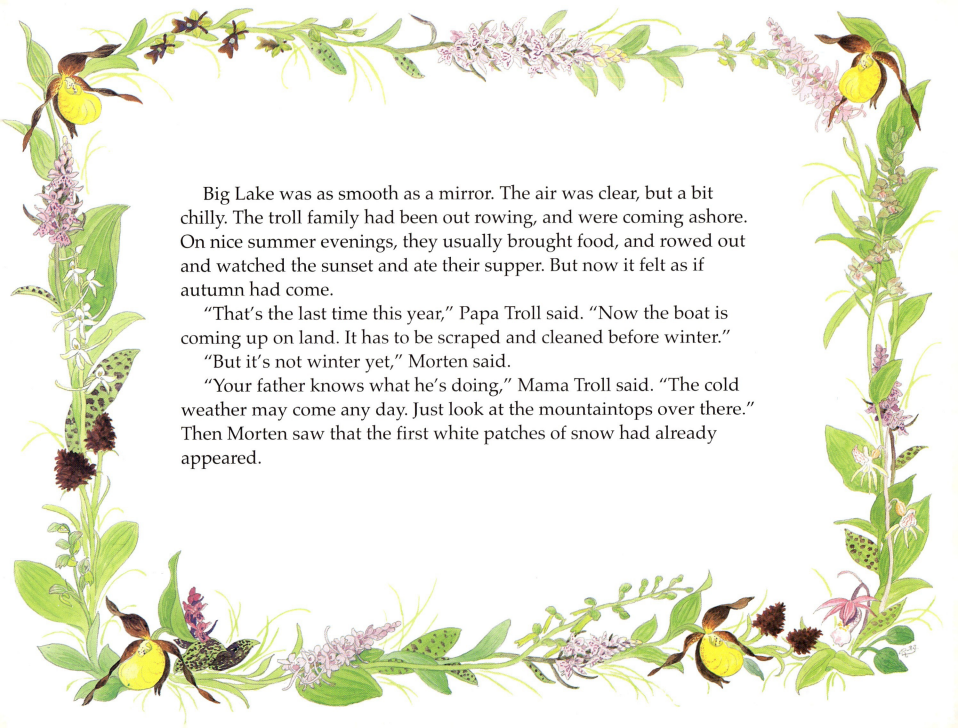

Big Lake was as smooth as a mirror. The air was clear, but a bit chilly. The troll family had been out rowing, and were coming ashore. On nice summer evenings, they usually brought food, and rowed out and watched the sunset and ate their supper. But now it felt as if autumn had come.

"That's the last time this year," Papa Troll said. "Now the boat is coming up on land. It has to be scraped and cleaned before winter."

"But it's not winter yet," Morten said.

"Your father knows what he's doing," Mama Troll said. "The cold weather may come any day. Just look at the mountaintops over there." Then Morten saw that the first white patches of snow had already appeared.

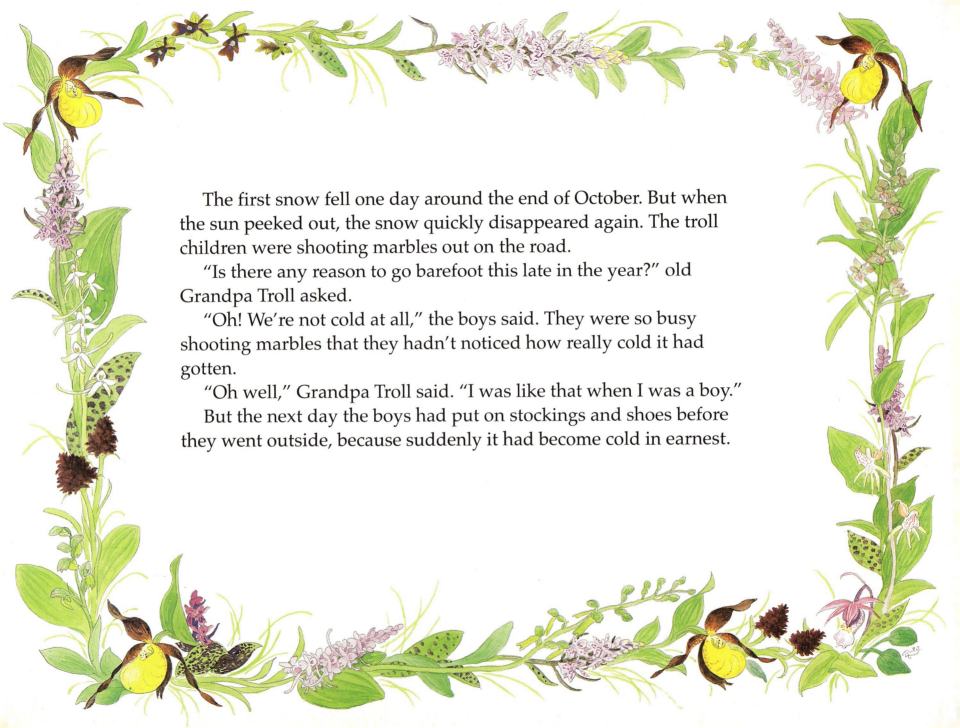

The first snow fell one day around the end of October. But when the sun peeked out, the snow quickly disappeared again. The troll children were shooting marbles out on the road.

"Is there any reason to go barefoot this late in the year?" old Grandpa Troll asked.

"Oh! We're not cold at all," the boys said. They were so busy shooting marbles that they hadn't noticed how really cold it had gotten.

"Oh well," Grandpa Troll said. "I was like that when I was a boy."

But the next day the boys had put on stockings and shoes before they went outside, because suddenly it had become cold in earnest.

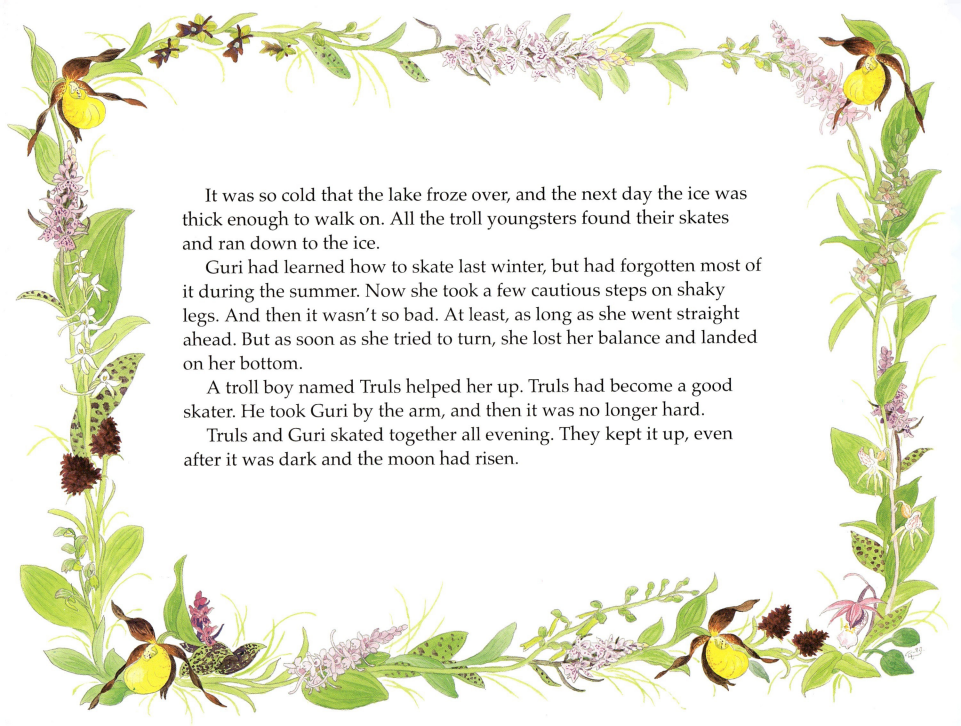

It was so cold that the lake froze over, and the next day the ice was thick enough to walk on. All the troll youngsters found their skates and ran down to the ice.

Guri had learned how to skate last winter, but had forgotten most of it during the summer. Now she took a few cautious steps on shaky legs. And then it wasn't so bad. At least, as long as she went straight ahead. But as soon as she tried to turn, she lost her balance and landed on her bottom.

A troll boy named Truls helped her up. Truls had become a good skater. He took Guri by the arm, and then it was no longer hard.

Truls and Guri skated together all evening. They kept it up, even after it was dark and the moon had risen.

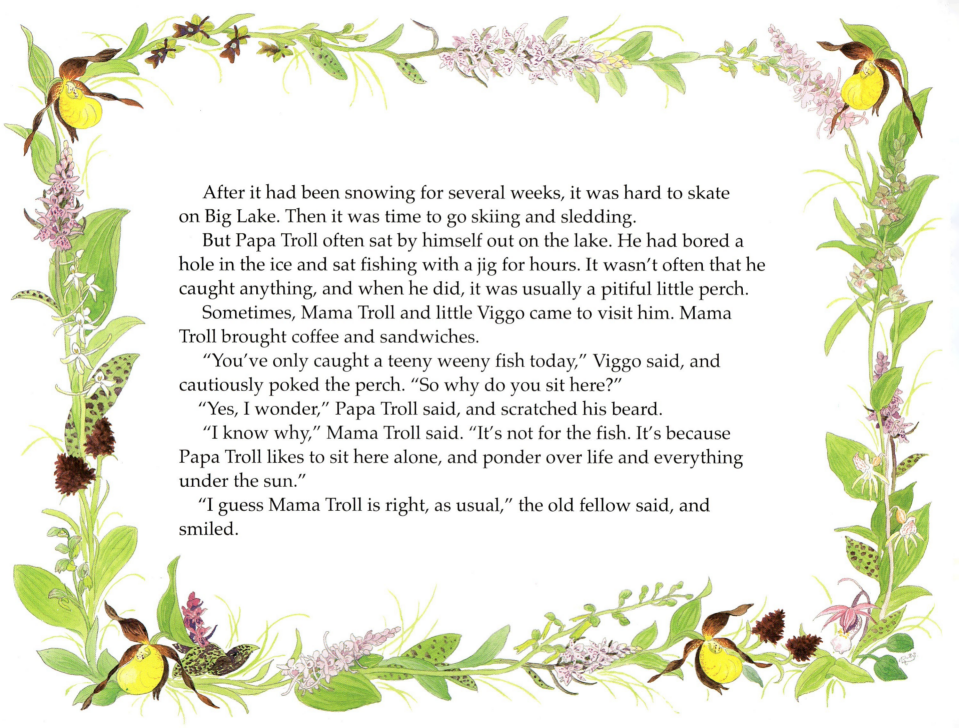

After it had been snowing for several weeks, it was hard to skate on Big Lake. Then it was time to go skiing and sledding.

But Papa Troll often sat by himself out on the lake. He had bored a hole in the ice and sat fishing with a jig for hours. It wasn't often that he caught anything, and when he did, it was usually a pitiful little perch.

Sometimes, Mama Troll and little Viggo came to visit him. Mama Troll brought coffee and sandwiches.

"You've only caught a teeny weeny fish today," Viggo said, and cautiously poked the perch. "So why do you sit here?"

"Yes, I wonder," Papa Troll said, and scratched his beard.

"I know why," Mama Troll said. "It's not for the fish. It's because Papa Troll likes to sit here alone, and ponder over life and everything under the sun."

"I guess Mama Troll is right, as usual," the old fellow said, and smiled.

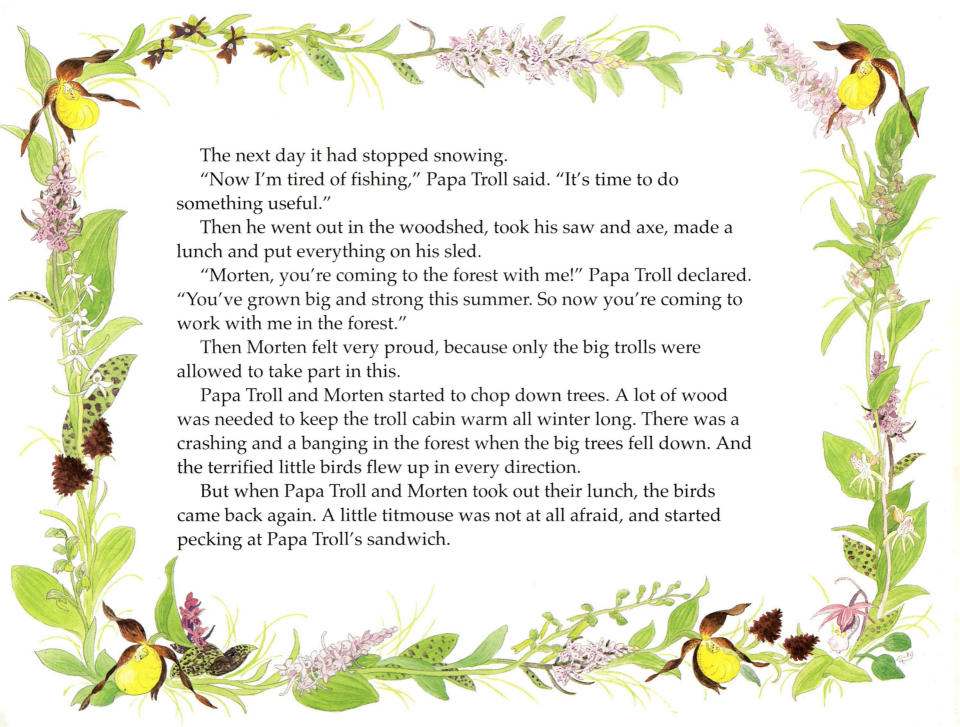

The next day it had stopped snowing.

"Now I'm tired of fishing," Papa Troll said. "It's time to do something useful."

Then he went out in the woodshed, took his saw and axe, made a lunch and put everything on his sled.

"Morten, you're coming to the forest with me!" Papa Troll declared. "You've grown big and strong this summer. So now you're coming to work with me in the forest."

Then Morten felt very proud, because only the big trolls were allowed to take part in this.

Papa Troll and Morten started to chop down trees. A lot of wood was needed to keep the troll cabin warm all winter long. There was a crashing and a banging in the forest when the big trees fell down. And the terrified little birds flew up in every direction.

But when Papa Troll and Morten took out their lunch, the birds came back again. A little titmouse was not at all afraid, and started pecking at Papa Troll's sandwich.

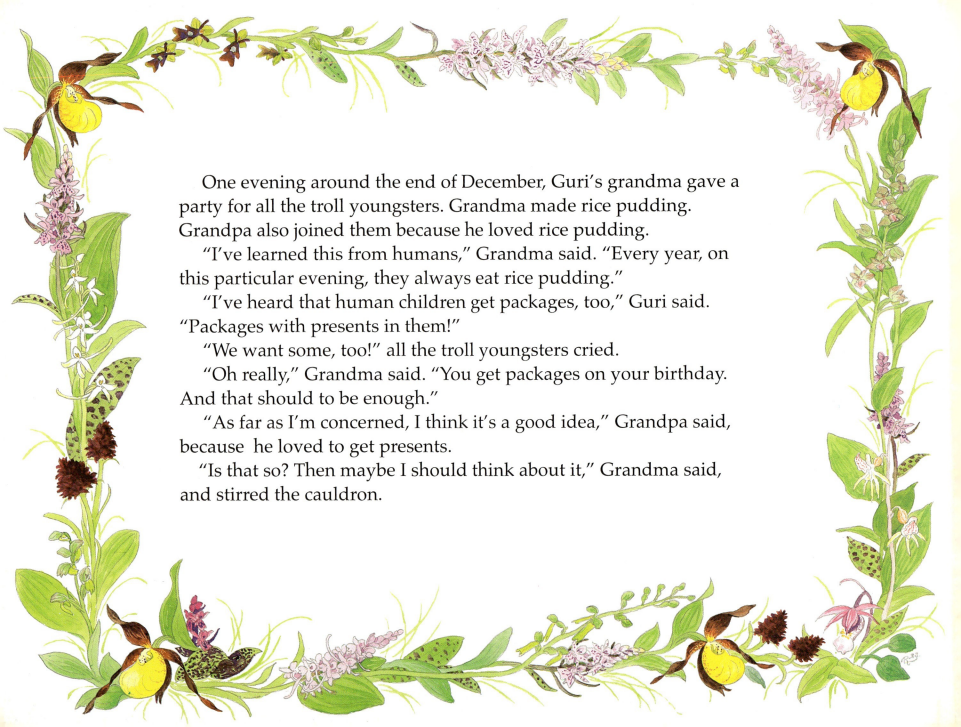

One evening around the end of December, Guri's grandma gave a party for all the troll youngsters. Grandma made rice pudding. Grandpa also joined them because he loved rice pudding.

"I've learned this from humans," Grandma said. "Every year, on this particular evening, they always eat rice pudding."

"I've heard that human children get packages, too," Guri said. "Packages with presents in them!"

"We want some, too!" all the troll youngsters cried.

"Oh really," Grandma said. "You get packages on your birthday. And that should to be enough."

"As far as I'm concerned, I think it's a good idea," Grandpa said, because he loved to get presents.

"Is that so? Then maybe I should think about it," Grandma said, and stirred the cauldron.

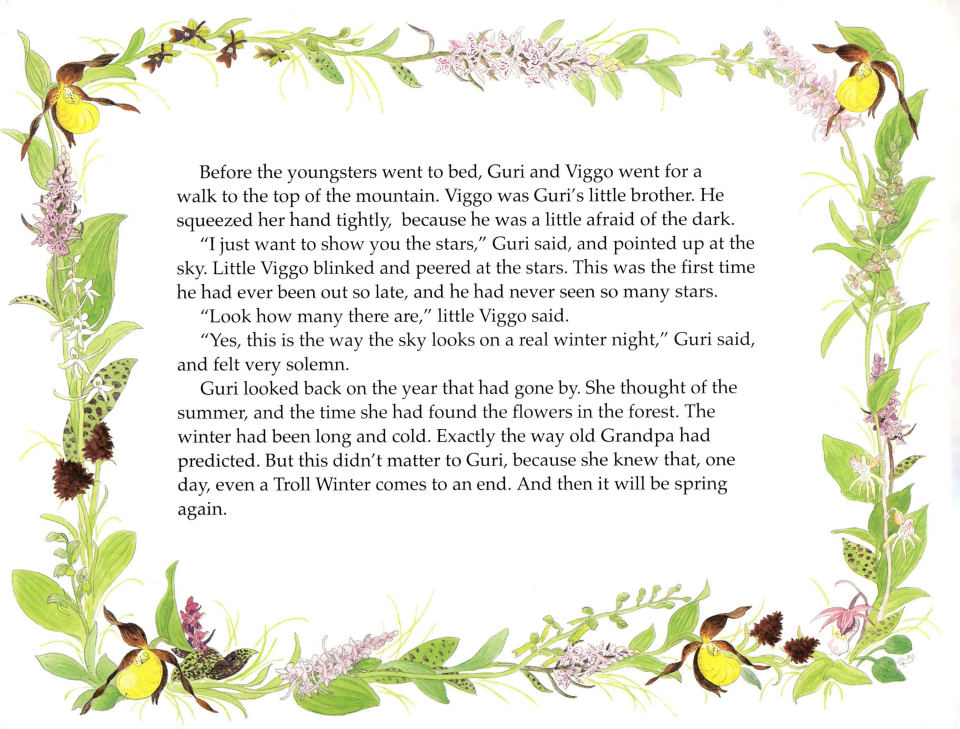

Before the youngsters went to bed, Guri and Viggo went for a walk to the top of the mountain. Viggo was Guri's little brother. He squeezed her hand tightly, because he was a little afraid of the dark.

"I just want to show you the stars," Guri said, and pointed up at the sky. Little Viggo blinked and peered at the stars. This was the first time he had ever been out so late, and he had never seen so many stars.

"Look how many there are," little Viggo said.

"Yes, this is the way the sky looks on a real winter night," Guri said, and felt very solemn.

Guri looked back on the year that had gone by. She thought of the summer, and the time she had found the flowers in the forest. The winter had been long and cold. Exactly the way old Grandpa had predicted. But this didn't matter to Guri, because she knew that, one day, even a Troll Winter comes to an end. And then it will be spring again.